MW01173833

WORLD ABOUT US
SOLAR
POWER

M. SPENCE

GLOUCESTER PRESS
London New York Toronto Sydney

© Aladdin Books Ltd 1992

Designed and produced by
Aladdin Books Ltd
28 Percy Street
London W1P 9FF

First published in
Great Britain in 1992 by
Franklin Watts Ltd
96 Leonard Street
London EC2A 4RH

Design: David West
          Children's
          Book Design
Designer: Stephen
          Woosnam-Savage
Editor: Fiona Robertson
Consultant: Brian Price,
          Pollution Consultant
Illustrator: Mike Lacy

Printed in Belgium
All rights reserved
A CIP catalogue record for this
book is available from the
British Library.

ISBN 0 7496 0803 X

Contents

What is solar power?
4
The Sun
6
Solar power today
8
Solar ponds
10
Power stations
12
Solar furnaces
14
Solar cells
16
Power in space
18
Solar cells in use
20
Cars and planes
22
Future in space
24
AD 2000 onwards
26
Fact file
28
Glossary
31
Index
32

Introduction

All living things need energy. The Sun provides us with more than enough energy to survive. For thousands of years people have used the Sun's energy to heat their homes. Today we are developing more ways of collecting this energy to heat our water and provide us with electricity. Using the Sun's energy as a source of power is called solar power.

What is solar power?

Solar power uses energy from the Sun to make electricity or heat. This energy reaches the Earth in the form of heat or light, which can both be collected and used to produce power. The Sun is also the indirect source of other forms of energy. The fossil fuels which we use today are the buried remains of plants and animals which needed the Sun's energy to grow. When fossil fuels are burned, this trapped energy is released as heat.

Photosynthesis
Photosynthesis uses the Sun's energy to change carbon dioxide and water into simple sugars. Plants need these sugars to grow.

Sun's energy

Carbon dioxide

Oxygen

Simple sugars (carbohydrates)
Water

Green plants use the Sun's light to make them grow. When we eat foods like meat, eggs or milk, we are getting the energy from the grass or other food that the animal ate.

Greenhouses use the Sun's heat. When heat passes through the glass, some of it is trapped. This keeps the inside of the greenhouse warm.

The energy from the Sun that falls on the Earth in just two weeks is the same as the amount of energy in all the world's supplies of coal, oil and gas.

The Sun

In just one hour, the Sun pours as much energy onto the Earth as we use in a whole year. Situated about 150 million km from Earth, the Sun is the source of almost all the energy on our planet. When its energy reaches the Earth's atmosphere, some is reflected straight back into space, and some is taken in by the atmosphere. The rest reaches the Earth's surface as heat and light, which are vital to our survival.

Creating heat
The Sun's rays are not actually hot. However, they warm up what-ever they touch by making the tiny particles which every-thing is made of begin to move. As the particles move faster and faster, more heat is produced.

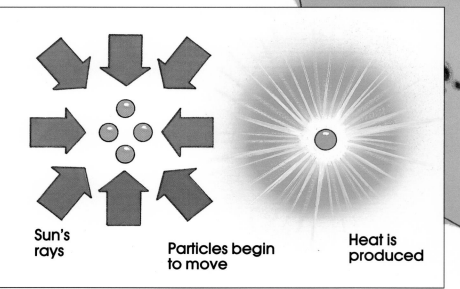

Sun's rays

Particles begin to move

Heat is produced

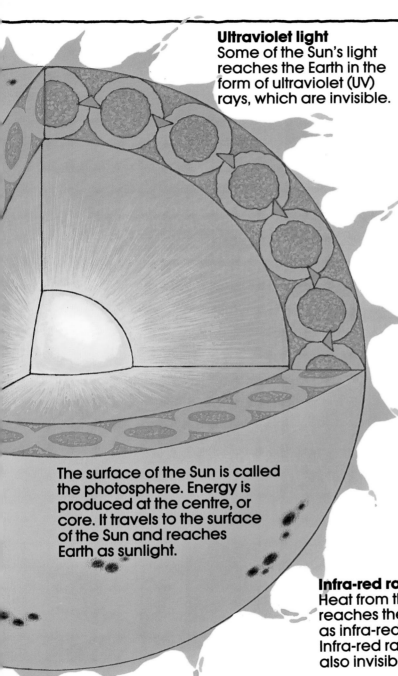

Ultraviolet light
Some of the Sun's light reaches the Earth in the form of ultraviolet (UV) rays, which are invisible.

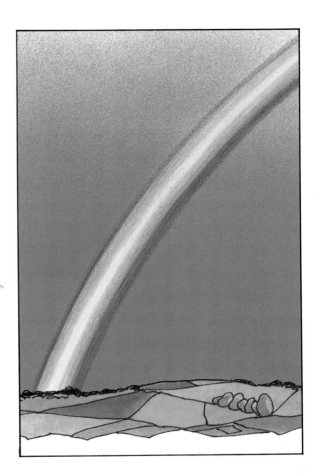

The surface of the Sun is called the photosphere. Energy is produced at the centre, or core. It travels to the surface of the Sun and reaches Earth as sunlight.

Infra-red rays
Heat from the Sun reaches the Earth as infra-red rays. Infra-red rays are also invisible.

Visible light
The light that we see on Earth from the Sun appears to be white. In fact, it is made up of many different colours. These colours can sometimes be seen in a rainbow (above). When sunlight shines through raindrops, it breaks up into different colours.

Solar power today

Today many houses can be changed to use the Sun's energy. Very simple solar collectors called "flat plate" collectors can be fitted to the roof. They are made from a shallow, rectangular box covered with glass. The box is painted black on the inside because black surfaces absorb heat very easily. Cold water is pumped through tubes in front of the black surface and is warmed up. The hot water can be used for washing or cooking.

One problem with solar collectors is that they cannot be used at night when hot water is most needed.

Trapping the heat
A solar collector works rather like a small greenhouse. Sunshine warms the plate and heats up the water as it passes through pipes. The sheet of glass covering the box allows sunshine in, and traps enough heat to keep the plate warm.

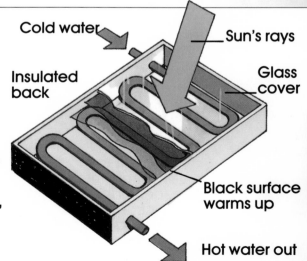

Cold water

Sun's rays

Insulated back

Glass cover

Black surface warms up

Hot water out

White and other light colours reflect the heat, which is why people in hot countries often wear light-coloured clothes. Dark colours take in heat and warm up quickly.

Solar collectors are often fitted onto south-facing roofs, which are very sunny. The sides and back of the collector must be made from special materials which stop heat escaping. This is called insulation.

Solar ponds

Unlike flat plate collectors, solar ponds can trap and store heat long after the Sun has set. The pond has sloping sides and a flat bottom painted black. It is partly filled with very salty water, called brine, and then fresh water is added. Sunlight heats the black surface and raises the temperature of the brine to about 90°C. The heat is trapped because the brine is heavier than the fresh water on top and cannot rise.

The sun can be used to turn sea water into drinking water. Sea water is poured into glass-covered tanks. The Sun's heat makes the water evaporate. It rises and cools back into water on the glass. The salt is left in the tank and the fresh water runs off at the side.

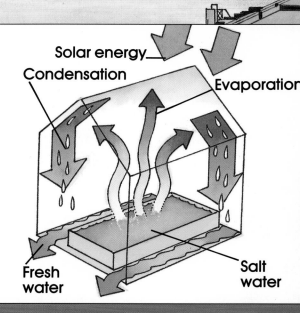

Solar energy

Condensation

Evaporation

Fresh water

Salt water

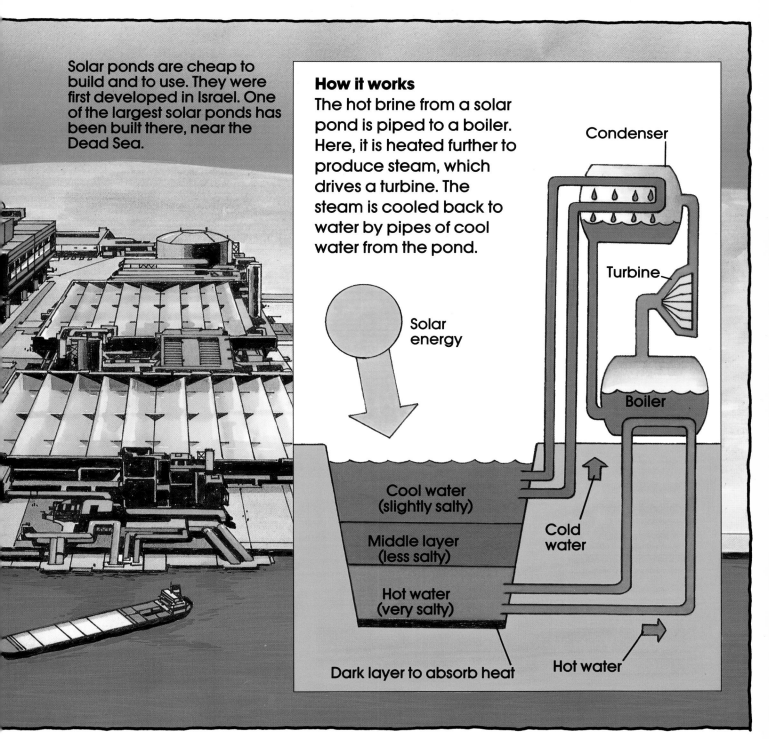

Solar ponds are cheap to build and to use. They were first developed in Israel. One of the largest solar ponds has been built there, near the Dead Sea.

How it works

The hot brine from a solar pond is piped to a boiler. Here, it is heated further to produce steam, which drives a turbine. The steam is cooled back to water by pipes of cool water from the pond.

Condenser

Turbine

Boiler

Solar energy

Cool water (slightly salty)

Middle layer (less salty)

Hot water (very salty)

Cold water

Hot water

Dark layer to absorb heat

Power stations

There are two types of solar power station. A central receiving station, or "power tower", uses thousands of mirrors, called heliostats, to focus sunlight onto a boiler at the top of a 78-metre high tower. Oil in the boiler heats up and is piped to a power plant where it heats water to over 300°C. The water turns to steam, which drives a generator. The second type is a distributed collector system. It also uses mirrors, and collects the Sun's light over a very wide area.

The heliostats
The mirrors used in both types of power station must have a completely smooth surface to catch as much of the Sun's light as possible. They must also be free to move and yet able to withstand high winds.

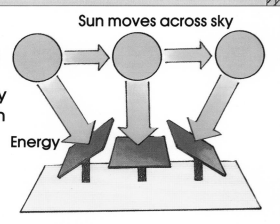

Sun moves across sky

Energy

Mirrors move to track the Sun

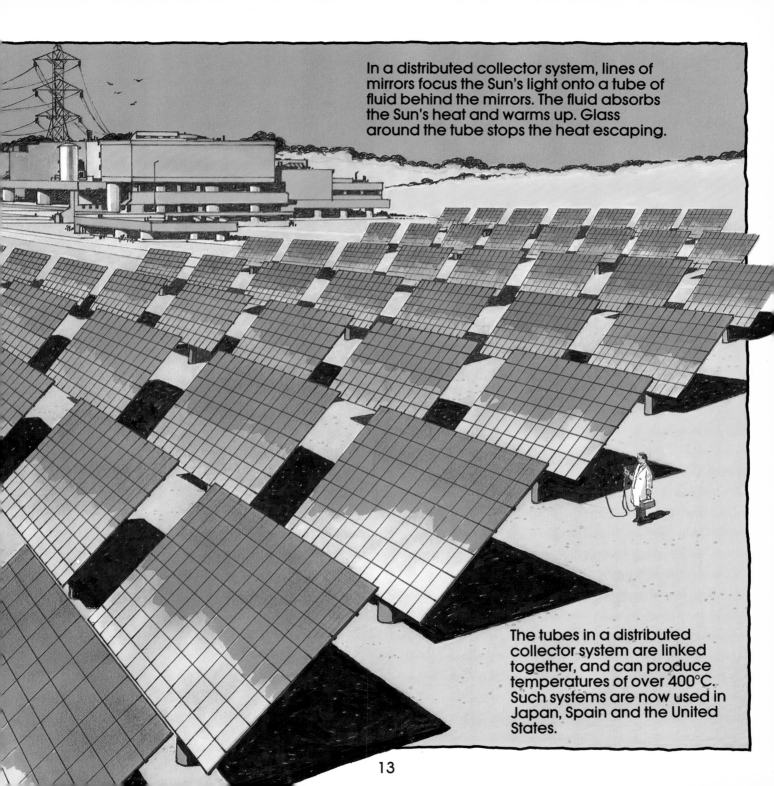

In a distributed collector system, lines of mirrors focus the Sun's light onto a tube of fluid behind the mirrors. The fluid absorbs the Sun's heat and warms up. Glass around the tube stops the heat escaping.

The tubes in a distributed collector system are linked together, and can produce temperatures of over 400°C. Such systems are now used in Japan, Spain and the United States.

Solar furnaces

Solar furnaces also use sunlight to raise temperatures. However, temperatures in a solar furnace are much hotter than those in a power station. The Sun is collected over a very wide area using movable mirrors. The most famous solar furnace is at Odeilo in France. It was built high up in the Pyrenees mountains to avoid the effects of smoke and pollution, which could block the Sun's rays and stop the furnace working properly.

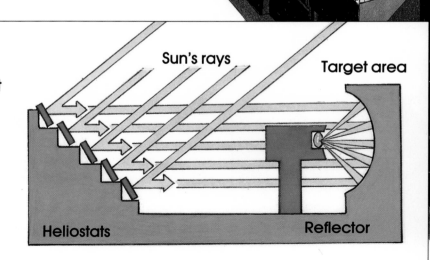

Working the mirrors
Thousands of flat mirrors follow the Sun. They reflect its rays onto a large, curved mirror situated opposite, called a parabolic reflector. The rays bounce off the reflector onto the target area, which sits in a tower in front of the reflector.

Sun's rays

Target area

Heliostats

Reflector

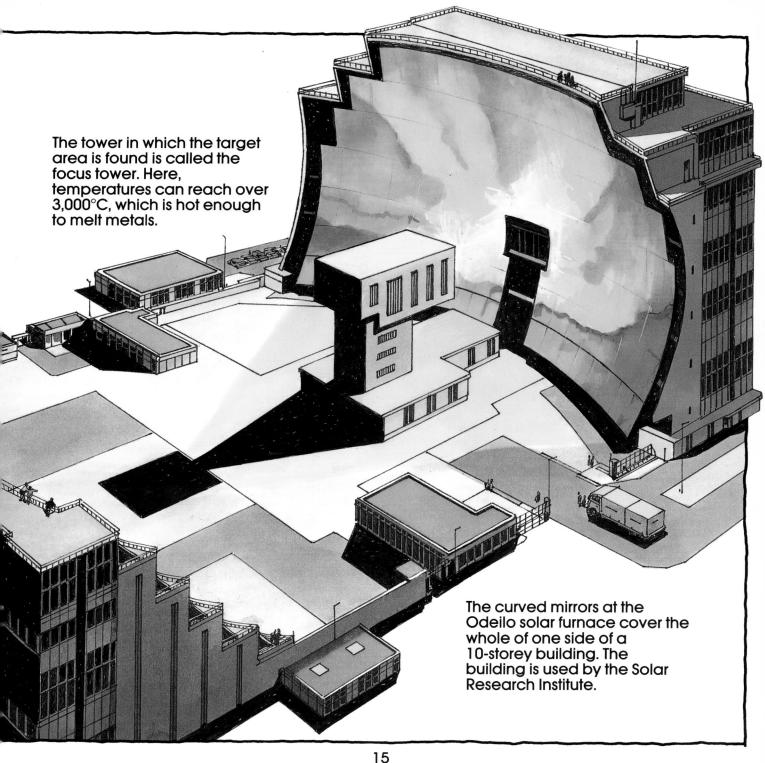

The tower in which the target area is found is called the focus tower. Here, temperatures can reach over 3,000°C, which is hot enough to melt metals.

The curved mirrors at the Odeilo solar furnace cover the whole of one side of a 10-storey building. The building is used by the Solar Research Institute.

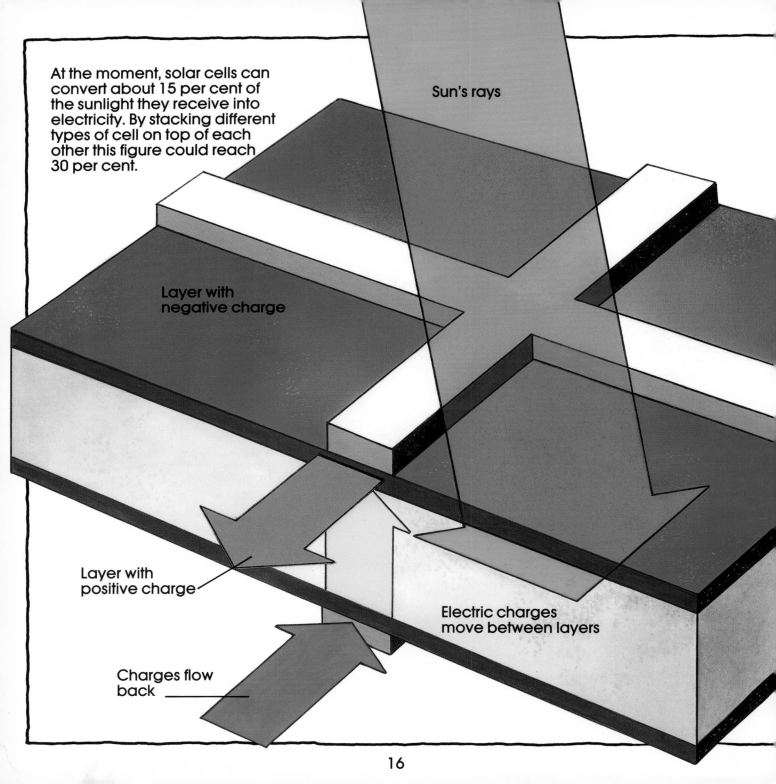

At the moment, solar cells can convert about 15 per cent of the sunlight they receive into electricity. By stacking different types of cell on top of each other this figure could reach 30 per cent.

Sun's rays

Layer with negative charge

Layer with positive charge

Electric charges move between layers

Charges flow back

Solar cells

Solar cells work just as well in cloudy weather as they do in sunlight. This makes them ideal for cooler countries like Britain. However, they do not work at night.

Unlike many other forms of solar power, solar cells use the Sun's light, not its heat, to make electricity. Solar cells work cleanly, safely and silently. They have no moving parts and need very little attention once they are in place. Most solar cells are made from silicon, which is found in sand and rocks. Silicon is cheap and there is plenty of it. However, it must be mined, which could be harmful to the environment.

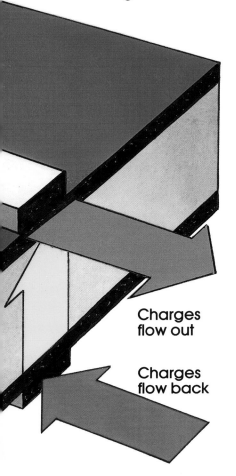

Charges flow out

Charges flow back

How the cells work
Solar cells are made up of two separate silicon layers, each of which contains an electric charge. When light hits the cell, the charges begin to move between the two layers. A small amount of electricity is produced, called a current.

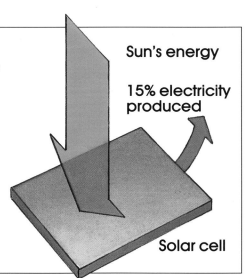

Sun's energy

15% electricity produced

Solar cell

Power in space

In 1959, Vanguard One was the first satellite in space to use solar cells. Solar cells work very well in space, where the Sun shines all the time and there is no atmosphere or clouds to block its rays. It is also difficult for satellites to refuel in space, and if they had to carry all their fuel with them, the satellites would be too heavy to take off! Moreover, the cost of the solar cells is quite small compared with the rest of the satellite.

The arms of the satellite are movable, which allows the solar cells to track the Sun as it moves through the sky.

After the success of the cells in space, research began into making them cheaper. They could then be considered for everyday use.

Many household items, like watches and calculators, now use solar cells. They are also found in lighthouses and in the buoys used by sailors out at sea. Panels of solar cells don't need much attention once they are working, so they are ideal for such uses.

Solar cells in use

As solar cells become cheaper, they are being used more and more. In remote places sources of energy are often limited. Solar cells are being used in such places to power water pumps, isolated telephone boxes and even railway signals. Individual systems of cells can either be fitted to houses, work-places or public buildings, or a "power station", which uses a collection of cells, can be installed in the village.

Cars and planes

In 1981 a plane called the Solar Challenger flew from Paris to England in 5 hours 20 minutes. It was powered by 16,000 solar cells on its wings and tail and was the first time the English Channel had been successfully crossed by a solar-powered aircraft. In 1986 a solar car named Sunrider travelled from Greece to Portugal using 300 solar cells. Solar cars must be very small and light. They travel very slowly, although they can cover long distances.

Cars can also be designed to use solar cells and a small motor. These cars are called hybrids.

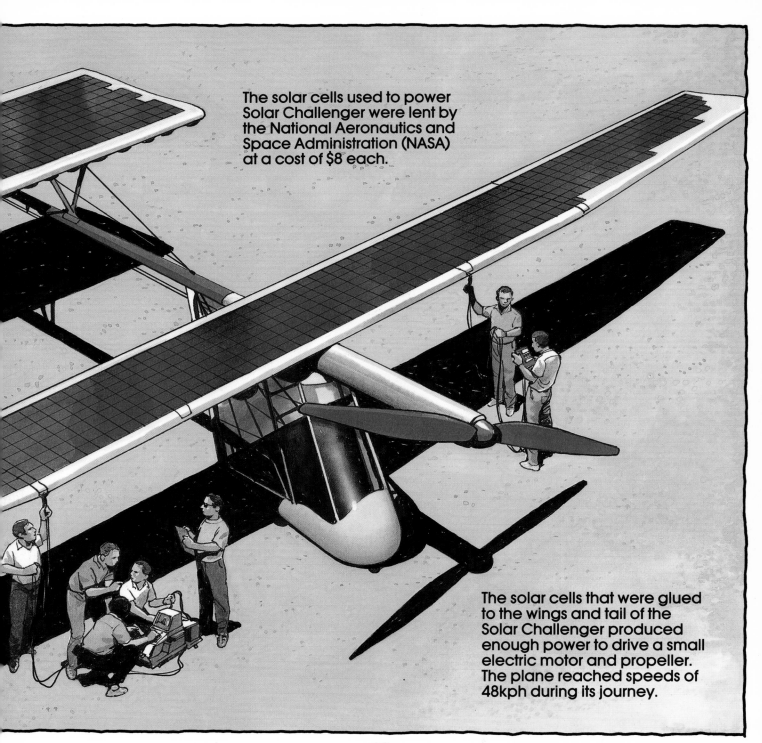

The solar cells used to power Solar Challenger were lent by the National Aeronautics and Space Administration (NASA) at a cost of $8 each.

The solar cells that were glued to the wings and tail of the Solar Challenger produced enough power to drive a small electric motor and propeller. The plane reached speeds of 48kph during its journey.

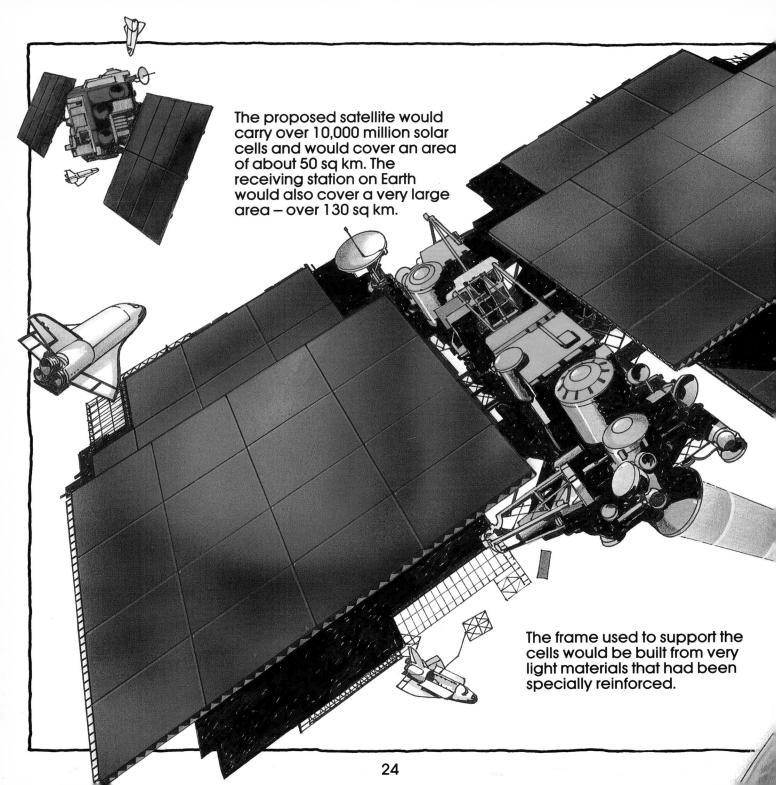

The proposed satellite would carry over 10,000 million solar cells and would cover an area of about 50 sq km. The receiving station on Earth would also cover a very large area – over 130 sq km.

The frame used to support the cells would be built from very light materials that had been specially reinforced.

24

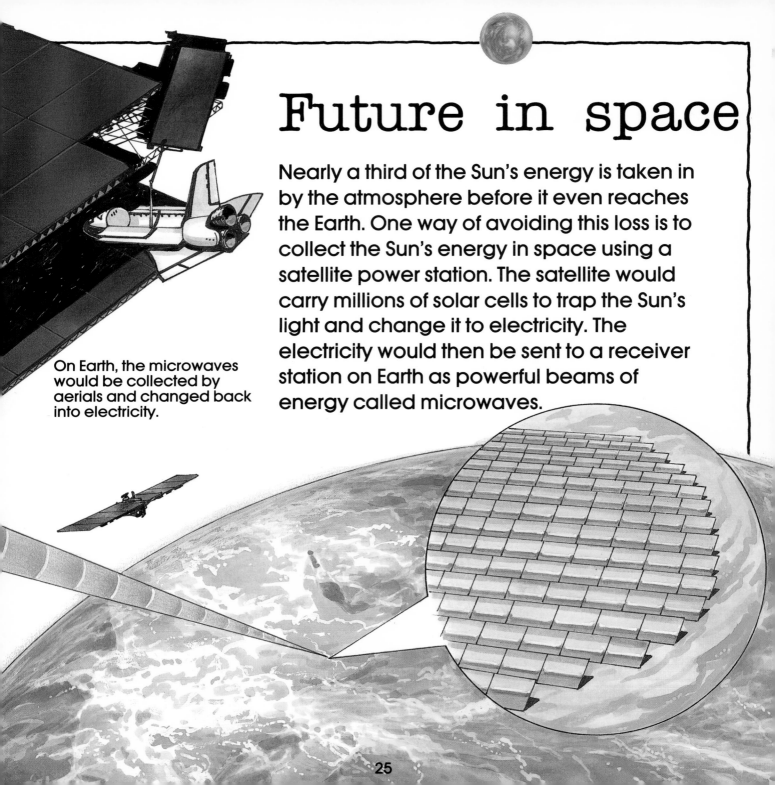

Future in space

Nearly a third of the Sun's energy is taken in by the atmosphere before it even reaches the Earth. One way of avoiding this loss is to collect the Sun's energy in space using a satellite power station. The satellite would carry millions of solar cells to trap the Sun's light and change it to electricity. The electricity would then be sent to a receiver station on Earth as powerful beams of energy called microwaves.

On Earth, the microwaves would be collected by aerials and changed back into electricity.

25

AD 2000 onwards

The Sun's power lies not just in its light and warmth. The Sun is also the source of other kinds of energy, such as wind, wave and water power. Like solar power, they also offer a clean source of power that will never run out. The process by which the Sun creates its energy, fusion, could also supply endless amounts of energy if it could be adapted to work safely on Earth.

Energy conservation, which means not wasting energy, will play a vital role in the future. Houses and cars will be specially designed to make full use of natural sources of power.

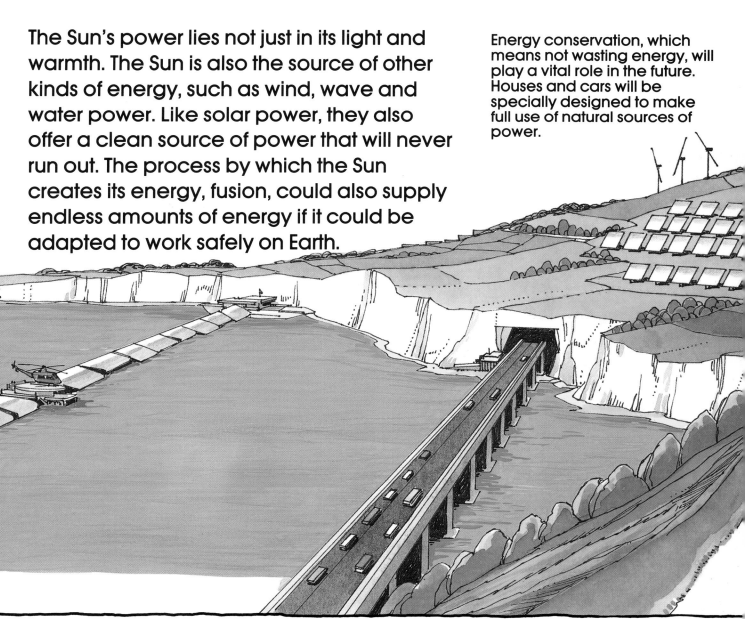

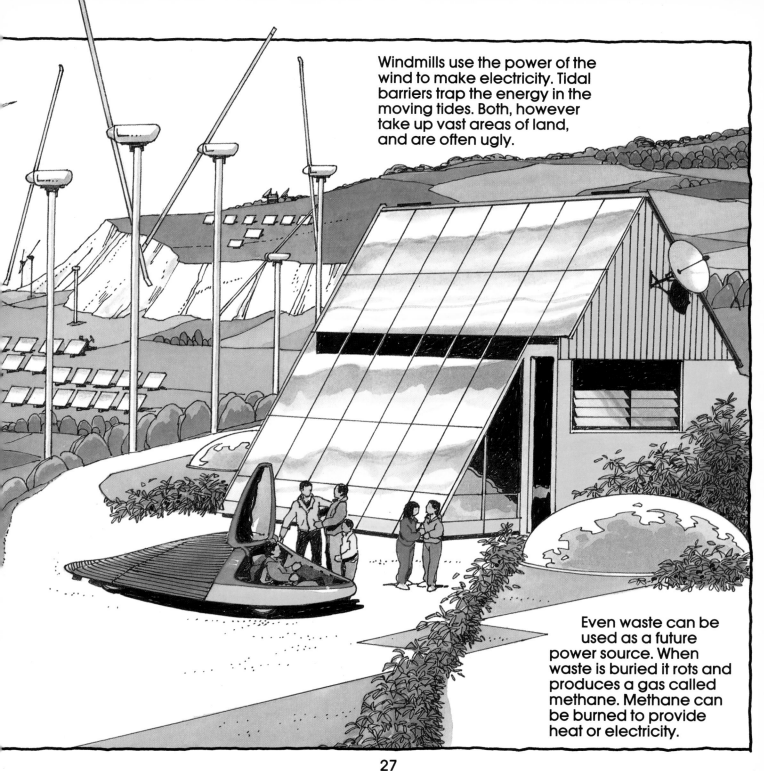

Windmills use the power of the wind to make electricity. Tidal barriers trap the energy in the moving tides. Both, however take up vast areas of land, and are often ugly.

Even waste can be used as a future power source. When waste is buried it rots and produces a gas called methane. Methane can be burned to provide heat or electricity.

Fact file

Solar cells were developed in the 1880s and were very expensive. They were improved in 1954 at the Bell Laboratories in the United States. The cells were very light and reliable, but were so expensive, they were used mainly in space. Today solar cells are much cheaper, and can last for up to 20 years.

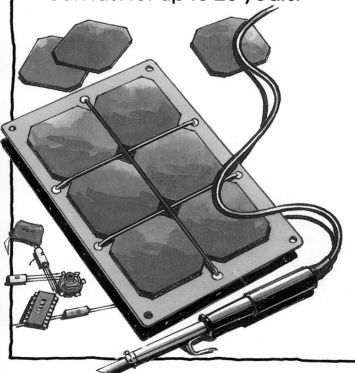

The distribution of solar energy throughout the world may appear to be very uneven (see map, page 30). In fact, the Sun pours enough energy onto the whole planet to operate 40,000 fan heaters – for each person! Even a cool country like Britain gets 80 times more energy from the Sun than it can use.

Greenhouses use the Sun's heat as a source of energy. Heat from the Sun travels to Earth as infrared rays (see page 7). The rays pass through the glass of the greenhouse and are taken up by the plants and soil inside. The glass prevents some of the heat escaping back into space and keeps the inside warm.

Many ways of producing solar power use the Sun's light, not its heat. In the future, it may be possible to use solar power at the North and South Poles where it is difficult to supply electricity. However, better ways of storing the energy must also be found during winter at the poles when the Sun never rises.

The world's first solar-powered hospital is in Mali, in Africa. Mali is situated on the edge of the Sahara desert, where there is always plenty of sunshine. Panels of solar cells supply the power needed to keep vital medical supplies cool in refrigerators, and to work other equipment, such as X-ray machines.

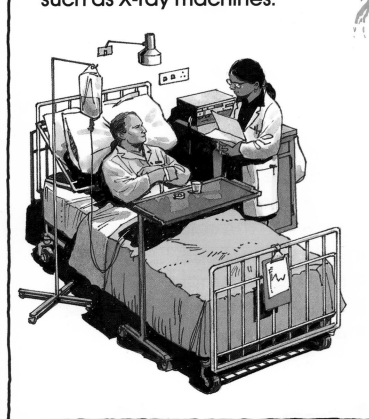

The map above shows how much sunshine each country receives during the year. Countries marked in red get the most sunshine, with temperatures reaching about 30°C during the summer months. They include Israel and parts of the United States, where solar power is already widely used.

Glossary

Brine
Water with salt added to it.

Condense
The name given to the process where water vapour turns back into a liquid as it cools.

Evaporate
The process of turning a liquid into a vapour. For example, when water is heated, it turns into steam.

Fossil fuels
Coal, oil and gas are the remains of living plants or animals which have been trapped or buried underground for millions of years. When they are burned, these fuels release the trapped energy as heat.

Heliostats
Lines of movable mirrors which follow the Sun through the sky and collect its energy.

Insulation
A material which is designed to stop heat passing through.

Reinforce
To make something stronger.

Silicon
A material which is found naturally in sand and rock. Silicon is plentiful on Earth and is used in solar cells.

Turbine
A device which turns to drive a generator. Generators can then produce electricity.

Index

B
brine 10, 11, 31

C
cars and planes 22-23
condensation 10, 31

E
electricity 16, 17, 27
energy 3, 4, 5, 6, 7, 25, 26, 27, 28, 29
evaporation 10, 31

F
fossil fuels 4, 5, 31

G
greenhouses 5, 29

H
heliostats 12, 14, 31

I
infra-red rays 7, 29

P
photosynthesis 4
power stations 12-13

S
satellites 18, 24, 25
solar cells 16-18, 20-4, 25, 28, 30
solar collectors 8, 9
solar furnaces 14-15
solar ponds 10-11
solar power 3, 4-5, 8-9, 29, 30
Sun 3, 4, 5, 6-7, 14, 18, 25, 26, 28

T
turbines 11, 31

U
ultraviolet rays 7